Brachiosaurus

Written by Rupert Oliver
Illustrated by Roger Payne

Library of Congress Cataloging in Publication Data

Oliver, Rupert.
  Brachiosaurus.

  Summary: Describes a day in the life of the long-necked Brachiosaurus and discusses its physical characteristics, habits, and natural environment.
  1. Brachiosaurus—Juvenile literature.
[1. Brachiosaurus.   2. Dinosaurs]   I. Payne, Roger, ill.
II. Title.
QE862.S3O44   1986   567.9'7   85-30051
ISBN 0-86592-219-5

Rourke Enterprises, Inc.
Vero Beach, FL 32964

Dimorphodon

Brachiosaurus

Dilophosaurus

Lystrosaurus

Rutiodon

Brachiosaurus

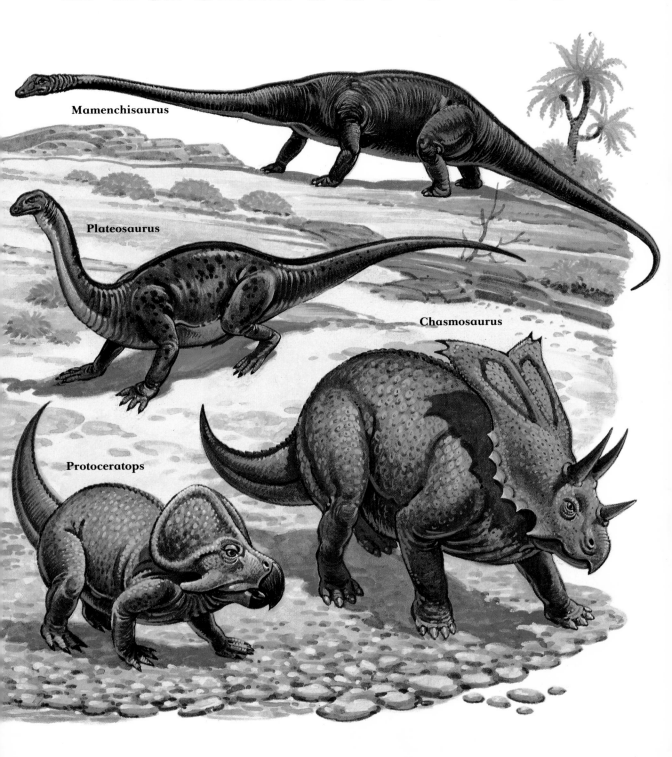

Mamenchisaurus

Plateosaurus

Chasmosaurus

Protoceratops

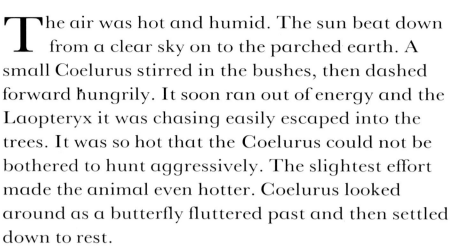

The air was hot and humid. The sun beat down from a clear sky on to the parched earth. A small Coelurus stirred in the bushes, then dashed forward hungrily. It soon ran out of energy and the Laopteryx it was chasing easily escaped into the trees. It was so hot that the Coelurus could not be bothered to hunt aggressively. The slightest effort made the animal even hotter. Coelurus looked around as a butterfly fluttered past and then settled down to rest.

High above Coelurus the swaying neck of Brachiosaurus reached high into the trees. She was looking for food among the high branches where other animals had eaten before her. The branches were stripped of all leaves.

Brachiosaurus was feeling the heat as well.
The glaring sun beat down upon her back and her
neck, making her feel uncomfortable. A slight breeze
stirred the branches and Brachiosaurus caught a
familiar and welcome scent of water. Wherever there
was water, Brachiosaurus knew, it would be cooler.
She set off in the direction of the water.

After pushing through the trees for a while, Brachiosaurus emerged on to the banks of a wide river. In the river, a young Camptosaurus and a Haplocanthosaurus wallowed in the mud. Brachiosaurus moved forward to join them. The mud looked cool and inviting.

Brachiosaurus rolled in the mud. It was beautifully cool compared with the hot, muggy air. Haplocanthosaurus must have felt cool enough, for it climbed out of the water and moved toward the trees. Then, the trees burst apart and a pair of Ceratosaurs leapt from the forest. The Haplocanthosaurus stopped in alarm. Ceratosaurs were fierce hunters and Haplocanthosaurus knew that danger was threatening. The plant eater turned to run, but the Ceratosaurs were too fast. Within seconds they had caught up with the dinosaur and were tearing into its soft flesh with their ferocious teeth and claws. It was not long before Haplocanthosaurus sank to the ground and the Ceratosaurs began their meal.

Brachiosaurus was worried. Ceratosaurs were as dangerous to her as to the unfortunate Haplocanthosaurus. She began to move off in the opposite direction. When a pack of Allosaurs suddenly appeared, she was frightened. Allosaurs were even bigger and fiercer than Ceratosaurs. Luckily, the Allosaurs were not interested in hunting, they had smelt the blood from Haplocanthosaurus. As Brachiosaurus backed away in alarm, the Allosaurs rushed toward the Ceratosaurs.

The Allosaurs began roaring loudly and displaying their teeth and claws. The Ceratosaurs were also displaying, but they were much smaller and not as powerful. As Brachiosaurus watched, one of the Allosaurs dashed forward and the Ceratosaurs ran away into the forest. The Allosaurs settled down to a stolen meal.

Brachiosaurus moved away from the river and away from the terrible hunters. It was still very hot and sultry, but a few clouds were beginning to appear in the sky. As Brachiosaurus pushed through the tall trees she disturbed a Dryosaurus and a Nanosaurus which had been chewing on some bushes. They scampered off for a short distance and then stopped. The air was so oppressive that the slightest movement was too much effort.

A distant roll of thunder reverberated through the air. Brachiosaurus stopped and looked around her. She shook her head in the still air. Then, the thunder boomed out again.

Quite suddenly the sky grew black as huge, dark clouds covered the sun. Lightning flashed across the sky, leaping from cloud to cloud and it became almost as dark as twilight.

Then, it began to rain in torrents. The rain was so heavy that Brachiosaurus could hardly see any distance at all and the forest around her dissolved into indistinct shapes hidden by the driving sheets of rain. Brachiosaurus felt the air cooling as the rain fell and the lightning flashed. It was a great relief after the oppressive heat, to feel cool water running down her neck and off her flanks.

Then, the rain stopped. Brachiosaurus looked around in surprise. In place of the gushing waters and dark skies of a moment earlier, there was bright sunshine. The ground underfoot was very wet and slippery and great pools of water lay all around. From the hillside a torrent of water ran down the slope toward the level ground. There had been so much rain that it could not soak into the ground and it was running off to find an outlet. The running water spread out when it reached the valley and Brachiosaurus could see that it had brought the body of an Othnielia with it. Perhaps the small dinosaur had been drowned in the sudden flood.

Brachiosaurus was moving off when a deep rumble made her turn in alarm. She had never heard such a sound before. It was not thunder. It sounded like no animal she had ever encountered. Then, as Brachiosaurus watched, the whole hillside seemed to twist and writhe. The rumbling grew louder as the soil, trees and plants on the hill crashed down into the valley. The heavy rain must have waterlogged the soil and undermined its hold on the hill. When the rumbling had stopped a jumble of fallen trees and mud spread around the foot of the hill.

Brachiosaurus realized just how hungry she was and looked around for some food. At a clump of trees not very far away, a Diplodocus was browsing on some of the lower branches. Perhaps there would be some good food there. Brachiosaurus moved toward the trees, passing a Stegosaurus on her way. The trees were full of tasty leaves and Brachiosaurus munched contentedly in the cool air which had followed the storm. It was no longer so hot and oppressive and Brachiosaurus felt much better.

Brachiosaurus and Late Jurassic Colorado

The Jurassic Period

The fossilized bones of Brachiosaurus have been found in rocks which are very old indeed. Scientists have managed to date these ancient rocks using a series of eras and periods. The Mesozoic Era, which means the era of middle life, began about 225 million years ago and ended about 65 million years ago. Scientists have divided this immense period of time into three periods. The first period is called the Triassic and lasted about 35 million years. The second period began 190 million years ago and ended about 130 million years ago. It is called the Jurassic period. The third period is known as the Cretaceous. The bones of Brachiosaurus have been found in rocks formed at the end of the Jurassic period. The dinosaur, therefore, lived about 140 million years ago.

The "Arm-Lizard"

Brachiosaurus means "arm-lizard" and scientists gave this dinosaur its name because of its peculiar bone structure. Its front legs were much longer than its hind legs, an unusual feature in the dinosaur world. Brachiosaurus belonged to the group of dinosaurs known as sauropods, one of the largest and most successful groups of the Age of Dinosaurs. Sauropods shared many characteristics in common. They were all plant eaters. They were all very large, and possibly grew up to 90 feet long. They all had long necks and tails. Most sauropods had hind legs which were longer than their front legs. Only Brachiosaurus and a few related species had longer forelegs. The reason for which has never been properly explained.

In the time when Brachiosaurus lived, the sauropods were the most important type of plant eater. There were more of them and they were larger than any other type of dinosaur. The lifestyle of the sauropods, however, has long been a source of disagreement among scientists. Even today, not all scientists agree as to how Brachiosaurus and other sauropods lived. This is due to the apparent inconsistencies of the skeleton. These creatures grew to an enormous size. It appeared that they could only support their weight by wallowing in water, much as hippopotami do today. Even if they walked on land, as is now believed, they could hardly have managed to move faster than a walk. Such slowness, combined with their lack of any weapons, left them wide open to attack by meat eaters. Under such conditions, their survival and success is puzzling. The tiny size of their mouths, compared with the size of their bodies, is another intriguing problem. It seems almost impossible that sauropods could eat enough to keep their vast bodies going, a situation which different scientists have used to try to prove a range of theories.

Skeleton of Brachiosaurus

Length: up to 90 feet
Height: up to 40 feet

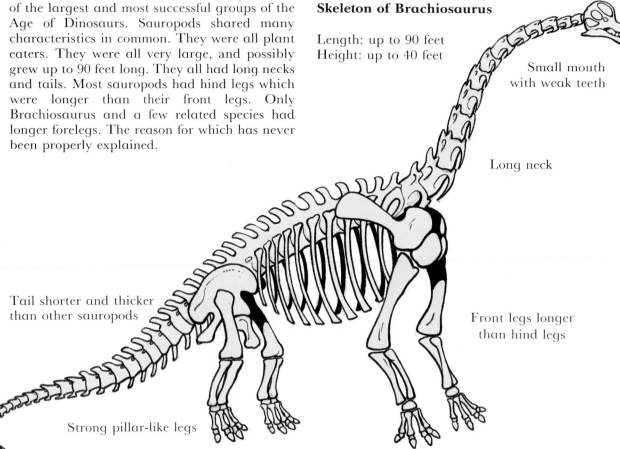

Small mouth with weak teeth

Long neck

Tail shorter and thicker than other sauropods

Front legs longer than hind legs

Strong pillar-like legs

Ornithopods which later replaced the sauropods as plant eaters

Parasaurolophus

Iguanodon

All in all, Brachiosaurus and its sauropod cousins are something of a puzzle. It can be stated that Brachiosaurus was one of the most massive animals ever to live on earth. In Morocco, Africa, scientists have found fossilized footprints of a dinosaur which would appear to have been 160 feet long. If so it would have been the largest animal ever.

Soon after this period, sauropods became increasingly rare as other dinosaurs took over their plant eating role.

The environment
In late Jurassic times Colorado was a very different place from the plain and mountain state which it is today. The Rocky Mountains had not yet formed and even the Great Plains were a thing of the future. The climate too was very different. Throughout the world, warm wet conditions predominated and the humid day of the story was not at all unusual. Some plants of the time would still be familiar today: redwoods, monkey puzzle trees and conifers were the most common trees. Ferns and horsetails carpeted the ground. Others, such as the cycads and tree ferns, would appear strange. Perhaps the most noticeable aspect of the Jurassic flora, however, is the absence of some types of plants. There were no flowering plants at all and no grass grew anywhere.

The animal life of the time was far removed from that of today. Mammals now dominate the land, but in late Jurassic times they were unimportant, rat-sized creatures. Birds, now common, were then clumsy fliers. It was the dinosaurs which ruled the world. The most important plant eaters were the sauropods such as Brachiosaurus, Diplodocus and the smaller Haplocanthosaurus. Other plant eaters included the small Dryosaurus, Nanosaurus and Othnielia, which belonged to the Hypsilophodont family. Hypsilophodonts may have been small, but they were very successful and managed to survive for more than a hundred million years after the time of our story. Camptosaurus, which can be seen in our story wallowing in the mud with Brachiosaurus, was the earliest of the large Ornithopods. Over the millions of years which followed, the various types of Ornithopod would gradually take over from the sauropods as the dominant plant eating dinosaurs. The line of the Stegosaurus, perhaps one of the most famous dinosaurs, would soon die out completely.

There were two distinct types of meat eater in the late Jurassic. The small agile hunters were represented by Coelurus, which caught smaller animals. The larger hunters included Allosaurus and Ceratosaurus. These probably hunted the larger dinosaurs, though some scientists see them simply as large scavengers.